FLOWER IN THE SNOW —HELEN'S STORY

LESLIE THOMAS

BALBOA
PRESS
A DIVISION OF HAY HOUSE

Balboa Press books may be ordered through booksellers or by contacting:

Balboa Press
A Division of Hay House
1663 Liberty Drive
Bloomington, IN 47403
www.balboapress.com
1 (877) 407-4847

Because of the dynamic nature of the Internet, any web addresses or links contained in this book may have changed since publication and may no longer be valid. The views expressed in this work are solely those of the author and do not necessarily reflect the views of the publisher, and the publisher hereby disclaims any responsibility for them.

The author of this book does not dispense medical advice or prescribe the use of any technique as a form of treatment for physical, emotional, or medical problems without the advice of a physician, either directly or indirectly. The intent of the author is only to offer information of a general nature to help you in your quest for emotional and spiritual well-being. In the event you use any of the information in this book for yourself, which is your constitutional right, the author and the publisher assume no responsibility for your actions.

Any people depicted in stock imagery provided by Thinkstock are models, and such images are being used for illustrative purposes only.
Certain stock imagery © Thinkstock.

Printed in the United States of America.

ISBN: 978-1-4525-9423-1 (sc)
ISBN: 978-1-4525-9421-7 (hc)
ISBN: 978-1-4525-9422-4 (e)

Library of Congress Control Number: 2014904379

Balboa Press rev. date: 03/26/2014

To Helen. Her never-ending love of life
has encouraged me to do the same.

Contents

INTRODUCTION

Inner wisdom is more important than wealth.
The more you spend it, the more you gain.
-Oprah Winfrey

I start this story with a confession. This confession tears me apart, but it helped to change a big part of my life.

When I first met Helen, I was leaving work a little later than I had planned. I am a teacher, and I had decided to check my mailbox in the workroom before I left, so that I wouldn't have to do it in the morning. Helen saw me and greeted me with the most sincere and heartfelt "Hello, how are you?" that I have ever heard. After that day I saw her frequently as I left school, and I looked forward to the small talk that we engaged in. I was having a difficult year, and her positivity consistently changed my mood before I left for home. She always made me feel better. She had this amazing bright light about her that beamed with intensity. Every time I saw her, I would be reminded again and again to be kind to other people and treat people like they are important, no matter how well I know them or what mood I happen to be in that day.

I asked what her name was, and she told me it was Helen. I noticed that she had on nice jewelry, and on closer inspection the next time I encountered her, I realized that it was *really* nice jewelry. She had on two diamond rings that were much bigger than the one diamond on my wedding ring. I wondered how a custodian could possibly afford such nice things. My ego concluded that they must be simulated stones, or that she must have made unwise financial decisions when buying jewelry, because she couldn't possibly afford them. I mean, how could she? Even worse than the judgments I was making about someone I didn't really know was my jealousy. I work hard, and my husband works hard, so why didn't I have expensive jewelry like the custodian?

I didn't run into Helen in the workroom for a while, and I just supposed that I was leaving at a different time, or that she must be working in a different part of the school. I asked some coworkers whether they had seen her around, and they had not. I made a concerted effort to leave school at the exact same time as I had before, so that I might bump into her in the workroom, but day after day she still wasn't there.

I finally gave up trying and stored Helen in that memory space where you store those people who made a difference to you. She was gone but not forgotten.

About a month later, I looked up one afternoon to see Helen walk into my classroom. Her custodial duties had been reassigned, and she had been moved from the workroom area to the gym, and now she was responsible for cleaning some of the upstairs classrooms after school each day. I was quite happy to see her, and I could tell by her smile that she was happy to see me. We exchanged small talk for a few days, and since it was nearing the end of the school year, she asked me what I was going to do for the summer. I told her that I was going to work on finishing my book. I said those words only to try and convince myself that I could accomplish what I had set out to do—write a book. I decided right then and there to make a statement to the universe. Her eyes got really big, and her smile got even bigger. I thought that she must be really impressed with me. It made me feel good. It made me feel that I wanted even more to finish my book. Little did I know that at that moment, the Universe gave a slight chuckle. It was determined to keep me on a course that would help me realize the things that are truly important in life. How could a custodian afford such nice jewelry? Indeed.

CHAPTER 1

Fun. Sad. Going on fun. Sad. Fun. Sad. Too many lives. Too many talks. Too many hurts. Too many everything. Where we go, what we do. I'm afraid I won't say things right. Somebody doing good. Somebody doing bad.

Hi, this is Helen. When I was four years old, I was just a little girl, and I lost my parents in the war. What a very sad thing. I lost my sister, and I lost my brother too.

Before I was born, my dad brought home food for everyone, but my older sister was so hungry that she ate her share and then ate my brother's share too. My brother was very hungry, but my dad thought he had gotten sick, so my dad borrowed money to get some herbal medicine. My brother didn't want to drink the medicine, and he said to my dad, "No, Daddy. No, Daddy, I don't want to drink it." But my father got mad and then made him drink it. My brother kept telling my dad that he was not sick but just hungry. But my dad made him drink the medicine anyway.

A short time later, my brother died. He had not been sick, just hungry, and I think the medicine hurt him. My dad got scared and told my mom she had to feed us more. He told her she needed to find fish, rice, and vegetables. He told her to find whatever she could.

When our bellies were full, my brother and sisters asked, "Why are we eating so much?" My dad just said he had a very sad story inside of him and didn't want it to happen again. I was so small, and everyone around me was so sad, but I was way too young. I really didn't know what was going on. I just kept jumping rope and playing around, living my life. I was just so young then.

After my brother died, my older sister cried and confessed she had eaten my brother's food. She told my dad she was sorry for eating all his food, but she was just so hungry. She told my dad she was the reason that my brother died. My daddy didn't know about any of this, and he had just buried my brother. My dad was so upset, and because of this news, he spanked her very badly. It was so bad that my sister ran away. All of this happened before I was born.

After she left, my dad felt so bad that he punished himself for it every day. After my sister grew up and came back to visit us, she told me she was just so mad about the war. She said my dad was angry at the war too. I think she felt bad about my brother, and she knew my dad was hurting too.

It is very painful to remember, but after the bomb hit and my mother was killed, my daddy must have been in shock, because he brought my mother's head to me. I took it because I didn't know what it was. It had long hair, and I turned it around and saw that it was my mother's face. I screamed and dropped it. Later, when we were at the funeral, I saw her casket was in a hole. I still wanted and needed my mom, and I was so hungry that I knew I wanted her milk, so I got closer and fell into the hole with her. I cut myself, and then someone put a ladder down there and brought me back up. I still have that scar on my head.

Later, when my father died from a helicopter bomb, there was no money to bury him. I didn't understand at the time, but my aunts, uncles, and sisters did not have enough money to bury him the way they had buried my mom. I was sad and didn't understand why he didn't have a casket, a real grave. They rubbed Chinese oils on him and then just wrapped him in blankets to bury him.

Sometimes when I think of my mom and dad, I get so sad, but I know they are around me. They have to be here to get me through my problems. My father was a very strong man, and he owned a farm. My mom was so petite, a very little woman. When my dad came home, the moon would just be coming up, and we would eat and laugh and talk. My mom would tell us that although our family was together, we were still missing one. I had no idea where my sister was, but I did know she had children.

When I was little, I got to go to prekindergarten, where I learned the alphabet. I was a curious child and always listened when people talked. One day I overheard my mom and dad talking about the fact that I had an older sister, one I had never met. But when I was around five years old, my sister came to visit us. She was married and had twin boys. She came to visit and brought her in-laws with her. She was so happy when she saw my aunt, uncle, cousins, neighbors, and everybody else, but she didn't understand why my parents weren't there. She didn't know that both my mom and my dad had been killed in the war. When they told her what happened, she was so sad and just started to cry.

I was so excited that she had come, and I was happy that she took me shopping for new clothes. It was a good day; I forgot about the sadness for a while. When we got home from shopping, someone wanted me to go babysit at a neighbor's house, so I went over to the house to take care of the little child. The baby was so big, and I was so small, that I dropped the baby. I got in trouble for doing that, but I told them I was too small and the baby was so big. I told them I didn't know how to take care of a baby.

I am not sure why, but in my family when you did something wrong, they just hit you. No discussing it, no talking, just hitting. I still don't know why. I just walked around with the baby, and I remember that I was sad and scared. I was sad because my mom and dad had died, and I didn't have anyone to help me, to be on my side. I didn't have anyone to comfort me or tell me everything was going to be all right. I didn't understand why people just hit me and never really talked to me. I remember thinking, *It's not like that in America. They have to be more responsible with a child.*

So far in my short life, everything had been very tragic. Both my mom and dad died from bombs in the war. My brother died from starvation. I still had a younger brother, and one day he and I were walking down the street. The constant rain had made the water in the street so high that it looked like a river. We walked carefully on the side of the street, but my brother was little and must have tripped or fallen, because he fell into the water. He just got washed away. After a couple of seconds, I couldn't even see him anymore. Everything in my life was very sad.

My older sister was so upset about losing both my mom and dad to the war that she left. She left me with my aunt and uncle, who lived two houses down from mine. They didn't want to have to feed me, and I heard them fighting about it. While they were arguing, I heard my name many times.

My sister's mother-in-law decided to take me somewhere. I had no idea where I was going, but she took me with her. She made me stay with some lady, and I had no idea who she was. She was a stranger to me. She gave the lady some money, and I stayed there for a little while. All I wanted to do was to go home, but I had no idea how to get home. I cried all the time because I was so homesick.

The lady would slap my face and hit me really hard every time I cried. She told me she wanted me to help take care of her baby. She asked me if I knew how to hold the baby, and I told her I didn't know how. I remembered the last time I had held a baby, and it wasn't easy. She made me do it anyway, and as I walked around, I tripped and fell. The baby dropped on the floor and started crying. The lady screamed at me, and then she hit me. She hit me really hard. It was awful.

I ran out of the house, and I realized I did know where I was. I walked home, which was about three houses down. I came home, and my sister fought with her mother-in-law about it. She should have told her mother-in-law I was too little and didn't know how to take care of a baby, but instead she didn't say anything. She just stayed quiet. I thought she would have protected me, but she remained silent.

After that, my aunt must have agreed to take care of me. My aunt already had a son, and I don't know exactly why, but her husband said he didn't want to keep me. He wanted to send me to my sister's house. They argued about it, and after much discussion, my oldest sister finally agreed to take me. She stayed at the house for about another week, and then she announced she was going to go back home, and she wanted me to go with her. I was happy that she wanted me and that I would have a stable home to go to.

We traveled a few days to get to her house. At first, everything was going very well, and I was very happy. My sister gave me clothes, she gave me food, and she even gave me some jewelry! I lived with her for a while, and then I went to live with other family members for a little while.

CHAPTER 2

Life is about moving. Moving me from
one house to another to another.

So I was moving again and went to go live with my oldest sister. She was married and had twin sons named Nathan and Nicolas. We traveled two or three days, and we had to take a boat to get to her house. It was really good at first, but she seemed to start having problems with her husband. They fought all the time, but because I was so young, I had no idea of what they were fighting about. One day she was so mad at her husband that she turned around and hit me. She hurt me very badly. She hit me with a belt, and I had cuts and bruises all over my body. I remember that I had more cuts and bruises on my bottom than anywhere else. I was really confused, because this was my sister! I really didn't understand what was going on. I just thought that she didn't love me anymore.

So in the middle of the night, I got up out of my bed, tiptoed out of the house, and just left. I just walked away in the dark and escaped from this place that didn't really feel like my home. I walked and walked. I had no idea where I was going, or what I should do. I just kept walking and walking all night long. Maybe my mother helped me along the way, I don't know. I walked all the way to Nha Trang. I didn't think about how far I had to go, I didn't think about the fact that I had no idea where I was or where I was going. I didn't think about any of that. I just kept telling myself that I needed to walk for two days and one night, and then I would be able to cross the ocean to go back home. I was too young to think ahead, to think about what was ahead of me. I just knew that I had to get out of that house, away from my sister, and I needed to just keep walking. I didn't think about bringing any extra clothes with me, or even any food or water.

The next morning I was exhausted, thirsty, and hungry. I walked around town looking for something to eat and drink. I was going down the middle of a street, and I found a piece of food that somebody had dropped. I could tell that it was dirty, but I picked it up and put in my mouth. I don't remember what it was that I ate, but I do remember that it tasted rotten and spoiled. I really needed to drink some water, so I looked around and discovered a hole in the sidewalk. There was water in the hole. I have no idea if it was rainwater, or maybe urine from a cow or other animal, but it looked like water. I just had to drink it. I don't remember what it tasted like, if it was good, or if it were spoiled. I do remember that it didn't smell good. I was so hungry and thirsty at that time, that I just knew it was food and something to drink.

So after I ate and drank, I decided to keep walking. I walked along, pretending to know where I was going. I just kept doing my own thing. I was so tired. I finally saw a house that had guava trees. I had guava trees at home, so I went up to the house and asked the person inside how long it would be until I reached the ocean. She told me that I was too young to be by myself and that I had no idea what I was doing. She asked me where my family was. I simply told her that I had to get to the ocean and that there was a boat that would take me to the other side. I insisted on telling her this, and I stayed strong. Unbelievably, I finally convinced her that if I could find the ocean, I would know where my house was. I had no idea, but I just had to make her believe me. She finally believed me and told me that she would help me.

She cleaned me up, fed me, and gave me a new shirt to wear. Then she actually gave me a little money. She brought me to the bus and showed me how to keep my money safe in my pocket. She took me to where the bus would pick me up, found the bus I needed, and talked to the driver. I rode on that bus for about an hour. I had no idea where I was going, or in what direction. Finally, I saw the ocean, and I told the bus driver to stop and take me down to it.

I got off the bus, walked down to the sand, and just sat all day. I waited and waited, but I did not see any boats. I didn't know the difference between a beach and a place where boats would let people on and off. I got tired and saw a man and woman that were probably homeless, but they were eating. I walked up to them boldly, and they asked me what I wanted. I just told them that I needed to get to the "big ocean" so I could get on a boat and go home. I told them that if I found the boat I needed, it would take me across the ocean, and I could then find my house. I told them that I knew where it was, and I knew how to get there if I could just find the boat. They just laughed and told me that I had no idea what I was talking about. They said, "You don't know nothing, girl. You will never get there." I was so desperate and hungry. I told the woman how hungry I was. She told me that I needed money if I wanted to eat. I remembered the money I had in my pocket, and I showed it to her. She took all the money and then gave me some food, but it was food that they had found on the ground or in a trash can, and it was rotten and dirty. I asked them to please help me get on the boat. I told them again that I needed to go on a boat for two days and one night, and then I would be home. They didn't listen to me. They had all of my money, and they turned around and left.

CHAPTER 3

I should say thank you to her to put all of that on me, so I can be very tough, so I can live my very tough life. Inside I die. Happy on outside. Nobody knows what is going on in my heart.

I was so frustrated, tired, and hungry that I just started crying. Another lady saw me and came up to me. She had three kids with her, and she asked me why I was crying. She asked why I was so tired. I told her that I just wanted to go home, but I could not find my boat. I told her that if I could just get to the boat, I could get home. I told her that all I wanted was for the boat to come, and I would ride on it for two days and one night, and then I could get off and find my home. She said that it was going to get dark soon, and that there was no boat coming. She told me that I couldn't wait on the beach anymore, because I was in the wrong place. She said that she had no idea how I got to the beach, but there was no way that I could get on a boat here. She said for me come home with her, and she would talk to the lady that she worked for, and that maybe they would know where I was supposed to go. She said her name was Lisa, and she was very nice, so I went home with her. It took only about fifteen minutes to walk to the house. She told me that this was where the children lived, that their names were Ken, Amy, and Elizabeth, and that she was their nanny.

When I got into the house, another woman was there. She said she was the children's mother, and she gave me a T-shirt to wear. It was so big that it went to my ankles. I can still see this shirt like it was yesterday. She said it was her husband's T-shirt, and that she wanted me to wear it so that she could wash my clothes, and I would be clean. She told me her name was Heather. She seemed really nice and told me that she was fun to be around. She talked about her kids and told me that one of them was about six years old, so I told her I was the same age. Then I laid my head down and slept until the next day.

I remember thinking when I woke up that this house was unfamiliar to me. I knew that I was not home. And I still wanted to go home. I walked out into the yard and saw kids playing. I went to see them, but I was behind a fence. I went up and touched the fence and knew that I could not get to the other side. A woman came out and asked who I was. She was the neighbor, and Ms. Lisa talked to her and said that I was lost, and that she had brought me here. Ms. Lisa took me back into the house and changed me back into my clothes that had been cleaned. I stayed in the house while the neighbors talked about me.

A few days later, I heard Lisa and Heather talking. I heard Heather say to Lisa, "I just might take her." Heather leaned over to me and asked, "Would you like to be adopted and live with me? Would you like to be my daughter?"

I had no idea of what to do. I just knew that she gave me food, cleaned me up, and was nice to me. She talked to me nicely and asked me why I had cuts and bruises all over my body. I told her about my sister and everything that had happened to me. All I can now remember her saying was, "Oh my God." It seemed like a clean house, a beautiful home, and a nice family. I liked my new brother and sisters, so I told her that I would like to live with her.

The next day they took me shopping for new clothes. Even though they were helping me, I still had it in my mind that I just wanted to go home. The problem was that I had no idea how to get home, and at such a young age, I could not figure out how to do it. The fact is that I didn't go home until I was forty-two years old. I never have found my three sisters. I don't know their names, where they are, or where they live;

I don't know anything about them. All I know is that my mom's name was Khanh and my dad's name was Le. I don't even remember my last name. My real name is Tang, which translates to "I will always win," and to me it means that if something hurts or troubles me, I still try to get through it, no matter what.

The rare times that I would talk about my real family, my adoptive mom would say, "Be quiet. You do not know anything." That really hurt me, because I wanted to talk about them, because I wanted my new family to know about them. One day my adoptive father asked me how old I was. I told him that I was six, and he declared, "You were born on December 10, and if you are six, you were born in 1959." After my adoptive father told me my birth date, he also told me that my new name translates to "a flower that stays in the snow." He said that I was strong, that I didn't run away from anything. He knew so little of me, but he did know how strong I had been so far. He just had no idea of how strong I was to be in the future.

CHAPTER 4

As days passed, I realized that I was not just a
foster kid, but that I was her servant.

From that time on, I had to work. I had to take care of everything for my new mom, for Heather. I was only six, but I had to do everything! My only role was to take care of my new mom. My mom and her family lived in an upstairs apartment above their grocery store. After I had lived with the family for just a few days, my mom took me down to the store, where I then spent most of my time. I would have to stay in the store by myself, with maybe an apple or an orange. She would lock me in, and I would have to sleep there by myself. She didn't take me back home. I would just eat my little bits of food and then go to sleep. No TV, no radio, no nothing. I was only six.

At night she would go upstairs with Amy, Ken, and her husband. She would just leave me there in the store by myself.

I couldn't cook, so she always gave me something cold to eat. They lived upstairs, and I lived in that store for a long time.

What would have happened if there was a fire or something like that? No one would have known I was there by myself. They didn't let me go outside or to see the neighborhood. Every day she just left me there, every day, every month. I was always scared. I was always nervous that something would happen. I am lucky that I am still alive.

I would cry so much that water wouldn't come out of my eyes anymore. Why would she do this to me? Why would she adopt me and then leave me by myself at night? That was so strange to me. I think she was a cold mother. I don't think she had any blood running through her veins. When I think about this, I get numb. I can't think anymore; I am numb. Who could possibly do this to a little girl?

When I was nine or ten, the family had to close the store. By this time, my mom had given birth to two more children, Diane and John. My mom brought me to the house to live, and I was so overjoyed. I thought that I would finally have some playmates, some friends. I thought that I was finally going to have a normal childhood. But, as it turned out, I was wrong. She put me in a quiet corner of the house, and I had to keep doing the same things that I was doing in the store. The first morning that I was in the house, my mother had clean clothes lined up for her children to wear. They ate some breakfast and then put on their clothes. They walked outside to go to school, and so I followed them. My mom immediately told me that I had to go back into the house; I was not allowed to go to school.

So I had to clean every day. Every day, every morning, every night, I just followed the nanny. Everywhere she went, I would go. Then later, as I grew up, I had to cook and to clean everything. I have to help her with everything in the house. All I was there for was to help her. I would just follow her and help her with anything and everything she needed help with. That is all I did. Day after day, week after week, month after month, year after year, up until I was about fifteen years old.

My mom at that time was about thirty-five, and she was still young. She still refused to let me go to school. I have no idea why. It's such a strange thing. She wouldn't let me go to school, and she never felt guilty about it. So I just realized that all I could do was to follow her and the nanny. I didn't talk or do anything that I was not supposed to do. When I did something wrong, or didn't do it the way she wanted me to, she would pinch me. She pinched me so hard that at night I would look under my clothes and find I had little bruises all over my body. I took care of her and the children, but I was not allowed to do anything else. I just worked, worked, and worked some more.

When I was younger, I remember my dad showed me how to wash the clothes with bleach. He showed me how he used his hands, but I was so little I couldn't do it. So I used my feet. I just jumped on the clothes and watched the dirt come out. My mom would not let me use the washer and dryer. I don't know why. I really wonder why. She had a machine to wash and dry the clothes, but she made me do it with my hands and feet. I had to wash her clothes, and my brother's and sister's clothes, and then hang each thing up on the line.

I had very long hair at that time. My mother would often take my hair in her hand and yank my head back. Sometimes she would do it because she was mad; sometimes it seemed like she did it for no reason. My brother was angry with my mom one night, and as I passed by him, he yanked my hair back. I couldn't believe it. He just did it and stared at me. I realized later in life that he did it only because he saw my mom do it, and he didn't know any better. He was always good to me, but this time I think he saw the hurt in my eyes.

In 1975 we moved to America. We moved to Minnesota, and it was very cold. I saw this as an opportunity to live in a civilized world and to have the freedom that I had heard about. My dad could speak English, but nobody else in the family knew enough English to even say, "Hello." I would see that her other children were going to school every day, and I would ask my mom if I could please go to school. She would just say no and make me work even harder. I was young; I wanted to play with my brothers and sisters and do the things that they were doing, but instead she told me to make her some tea or some soup. I was so young, and I had no idea what I was doing.

One day I didn't put a hot pad on the handle of the pot of soup, so when I went to serve it, the handle burned my hand, and I dropped the pot. The soup went down my arm and burned me very badly. My dad took me to the hospital, and they put cream on my arm. My dad took me home and started yelling at my mom. He said, "You cannot make her work; you cannot make her do all of this; you cannot continue to treat her this way," but she ignored him and just kept making me do things for her. It didn't matter what he said. She did not listen to him at all. I still have a big scar on my arm from that hot soup pouring on my arm.

At one point some neighbors saw that I wasn't going to school, and they called the police. My mom then had to let me go to school, but when I was there, I couldn't talk to anyone, because I still didn't know the language. I would just sit and cry. They probably thought something was wrong with me, but I was scared and didn't understand anything that was going on. I had been to school only when I was very young in

Vietnam, and that didn't last very long, because my parents had died. I was alone and I was scared. I didn't sleep very much, so I couldn't concentrate at all, and I had no patience.

But at least I got to go to school. The lady from the church then asked me how I was being treated, and I told her I was treated very badly. She took me away from my mom and gave me food and a place to sleep. The people in that home were all trying to talk to me, but I didn't speak much English. I hadn't had enough interaction with other people in America to learn the new language. The lady from church spoke Vietnamese, but she was the only one.

So after a few days, my mom got really mad and told my dad to go over to the house and bring me home. He spoke English well, and he told them that he was going to take me home, and that I would be well taken care of. I was so scared, and I didn't really know what to do, so I agreed to go home. I again lived with my adoptive parents. If I had stayed in that lady's house, today I would know how to read, and I would know how to write. When I got back home, my mom sang a song to me in Vietnamese that went something like this:

> I brought you to the United States,
> And you flew away, and I want to know why.
> You are a bird, and you will now stay in the cage.

So when I came back home, the next day my mom made me get up very early and make her some tea. I went to school, but when I got home, I immediately had to wash the clothes and the sheets by hand and do the housework. I worked so hard that my hands would bleed, and when I put them in the water, they would sting. After we moved to America, she had nobody to help her with this stuff—no more nanny to do some of the work—so she made me do all of it. I cried all of the time, and she would tell me that she was confused as to why I was crying. She would tell me that she wasn't going to do anything to me anymore. I would still cry. One day, I heard my dad tell her that she didn't know how to take care of me, and that she didn't know how to love me. She got very mad and slammed the door.

I wanted to be part of the family, but when we moved into the American house, my mom moved me into the basement right away. It was so dark at night, and I was very scared. I would turn on the lights, and she would yell at me to turn them off, because it cost too much money for the lights. So I waited until she was asleep, and I would turn a little light back on. She wouldn't let me sleep upstairs with everyone else. It was very cold in the winter in the basement, and it was always very dark and scary. When I would go down to the basement, I was supposed to sleep, but I was so scared that I couldn't close my eyes. Because I never slept at home, the only place I felt safe to sleep was at school. I was in a new place, a new house, and all I had to call my own was a dark, cold, basement. I would come home late and try to do my homework, but I lived in the basement, and I was so scared. I was also very tired. I would go to school the next day, and fall asleep, so my teacher called my mom and dad to tell them. My mom just said, "I don't know why she does this," and acted as if she had no clue why I was so tired, but she knew. My dad didn't know, so he just thought I was being lazy. He didn't know that I worked all the time and that I was too cold and scared to sleep at night.

One day I was eating, and my mom told me that she wanted me to do something for her. I said to her, "Can I do it after I eat?" and she jumped up and yelled and screamed at me. Everybody just stopped what they were doing and stared at her. Then they all turned toward me and just stared at me. I started to cry and got up and did what she wanted me to do. Nobody said a word. They just stared at me. I was so embarrassed.

Another time my mom asked me if I could do something for her the following day. I told her that the next day was Thanksgiving, and that every American stays home, makes a big meal, and doesn't go to work. She told me that she didn't care, and that I had to do it. I tried to explain to her that the stores would be closed because of Thanksgiving Day. She jumped up, went over to the radio, and turned the music up really, really loud. She started screaming at me to be respectful, to not talk back to her. I told her that I was sorry but that I felt like I didn't do anything wrong. I told her that I just wouldn't talk to her anymore. It seemed funny to me, but when her own son would talk back to her, she wouldn't do anything about it. But if I said anything to her, argued with her at all, gave her a weird look, she would scream at me. It just wasn't right; it isn't fair to treat your daughter that way. It isn't right to treat another human like that.

I did go to school from about the ninth to the twelfth grade, but for all those years, when I got out of school at three o'clock, I would go to work at the school cafeteria, or the library. Then I would go down to the local cafeteria and work some more. I would mop the floors and do whatever they needed me to do at the cafeteria. Then I would go into a little secret room in the cafeteria and sleep for a few hours. When I got a little older, I worked at Taco Bell for a while after school. Sometimes my dad would skip his lunch and come pick me up so that I didn't have to walk home. I felt like he was trying to be nice to me. I'm sure my mom didn't approve, and I wondered if she even knew that he was doing that for me.

CHAPTER 5

I am so petite. I was only seventy-nine pounds, and now I am fifty-three years old, I am only ninety-five pounds—maybe because I work so much I can't grow up? When I was a little girl, I had two baskets. One basket in the front, and one in the back. Then there is a stick that you put on your shoulder, and carry it around to the house. I always did that; I always carried that basket.

All through high school, I worked and worked. I went to school and then would go to a job after school. When I came home, I would work in my mom's house until very late, and then I would go down into the basement. I worked so hard every day; maybe that is why I weighed only seventy-nine pounds after high school. Maybe all of that working made me so small. Maybe I never really got a chance to grow.

After high school, my family moved down to Lubbock, Texas, and I got a job in a pancake house. After that I worked at a hotel for a long time. I worked and worked every day, and my sisters and brother went off to college. It was hard, so very hard for me to see that. I worked all the time, all those years, and watched my brothers and sisters grow. They learned American ways and became very smart. They were happy and playful. About the only conversation that I would have would be when my mother spoke to me. Most times she would make sounds like, "tick, tick, tick, tick"—like some kind of a signal to make sure I kept moving and working. She never really ever talked to me like a regular person.

Even though I was getting older, she constantly made me take care of everybody. She would make me clean and do everything for her, and the house. Other than my dad, I was the only one who worked at all. For many years I worked in a convenience store until two in the morning. I would come home from work and sleep a little, and then I would have to get up so that I could do things for her. When my brothers and sisters were all home, I would have to fix dinner for everyone, and then the family would sit down to eat together. I would have to wait until they were done, and then I was allowed to eat if there was anything left over. I was never allowed to eat with the family. The kids never asked me why, never wondered why I didn't eat with them. It was just how it was, and they had always grown up with that. It was normal to them.

CHAPTER 6

---

*I hope that one day my husband will love me and
change my destiny, to offset the lack of affection, as
well as sharing the sorrow that I have tasted.*

When I was twenty-four, I worked in a convenience store in
Lubbock. I worked all day and would try to take a nap now
and then in the cigarette room. They kept boxes and boxes of
cigarettes in one room, and it was cool and quiet. One day in
September of 1983, a man came into the store and talked to
me; he told me his name was Tung but his friends called him
Tony. He told me that he was helping a friend get a car. He
came by the store where I worked daily, to get a soda or some
chips. He would come back day after day and maybe buy
something, or maybe just stand by a shelf and look around.
He would buy cigarettes and get oil for an oil change (he told
me later that he didn't ever use it!) and things like that. He
would just keep his eye on me all the time.

So I thought he was suspicious-looking, and I told the police officers that came into the store every day. They watched him for a few days, but he never did try to rob me or the store. They told me that they thought he was a nice guy, and when the police found out later that he just wanted to see me at the store, they thought it was a beautiful story. Then one day Tony talked to my dad and told him that he wanted to marry me. He told my dad that he just fell in love with me. He talked to my mom and dad, and they introduced him to my brothers and sisters. He was very sweet, and spoke nicely. He would come by and help my dad and talk with my brothers and sisters. They would tell me, "Oh, he is very nice. Maybe he will marry you!"

I had never even been on a date before, and I was twenty-four years old. I was not allowed to go anywhere; I was not allowed to go out. We never went on a date, never went anywhere together. I wondered how he knew that he wanted to marry me, when he didn't know me. I asked him many questions, such as if he had a girlfriend or a wife. I asked if he had a family somewhere. He told me that he didn't even date anyone, that I was the only girl he talked to. I told him that I did not want that kind of life, and that if he had a family, then he needed to go home and leave me alone. I was trying to make sure that I did not get into a situation that I did not want. I wanted to make sure that everything was up front and honest. He told me that he wanted to get married, and he wanted to get married now. I told him that if he loved me, then he would wait for me. I told him that I wanted to marry someone older than I, and he told me that he was. He told me that he did not smoke, was a nice guy, loved my family, and would take care of my family and me forever. He told me he worked hard, had two jobs. He said he worked Monday through Friday, forty hours, and that he usually worked all weekend too. He was a nice guy, a very handsome guy. I told him that all I did was work. I told him that I didn't even know how to drive. I had to think about all of those things. I was not your normal girl, I'd had a pretty rough life, and didn't want to get into a worse situation. My older brother taught me how to drive, and I was happy that things were finally going my way.

I went home to tell my family that Tony wanted to marry me, and my brothers and sisters got so excited. They asked me if he had a car, and I told them that he did. They told me that I should marry him so that he could drive us all around. They did not have a car to drive and got very excited that they could go to the mall or to the movies in Tony's car. That is when I decided that I should just go ahead and marry him. How silly was that?

Tony and I got married on March 10, 1984. After I got married, my mother had to get a job and start working, because I wasn't there anymore to provide an income for her. Everything was going so well, and the next year I had a baby. I was so happy that I had a son. We named him Anthony. He was very healthy and was born on December 11, 1984. We were happy and having fun, and I would say to myself that I finally was going to be able to have a good future, and a wonderful life.

So I was living a good life. I was happy, doing well, and we were thriving. I had a loving husband, a beautiful son. We worked so hard, and I bought and ran a nail salon. We bought a beautiful house. Then one day we were talking about life and our plans, and Tony told me that he had once had a girl in Vietnam that he wanted to marry.

At that time, he had decided to go to a palm reader, and the palm reader told him that if he married that girl, his father would die. So his family got scared and, he said, stopped him from marrying her. I appreciated that he told me all of this, and I felt closer to him. Then one day when I was cleaning, I moved some books from a shelf. Something dropped on the floor, and I picked it up and saw that it was a letter. Since I can't read, I took the letter to my mom's house, and she read it for me. The letter said that my husband had been married, and that he had a son. I just hid the letter; I was so embarrassed and angry. I think that was the day that my heart died. So he had lied to me. He did marry that woman, and he had a son.

I really didn't know what to do at that point. At first I was so angry that I told myself that I would confront him with this discovery. I would show him the letter and make him tell me why he had lied to me about this. Why did he even tell me the story, and then lie about what had really happened? When I got home, I started to go to him and talk about it. Then I turned around and realized, *I am married to him now, I have a beautiful son named Anthony, and what good would it do to talk him about it?* I think that part of my heart died a little more then.

Things started to change after that. Tony was acting differently, not treating me the same way. One day he got angry at me and called me stupid. That hurt more than anything he could do to me. I just kept telling myself that he was going through a phase, that soon he would be back to his old self, and we would talk it out. Instead, Tony came home and told me that he was going to be gone a lot, because he was going to go to school. He said that he had decided to go to school for a year to be a mechanic. I told him that I didn't want to be married to a mechanic—really because he wanted his own shop, and I didn't want to work in a mechanic's shop. He fought with me and told me that there was no way that I would win this battle, so I had to let him do it. I told him that I would work somewhere else and just help him from home, but he told me that that wasn't how he wanted it, and that I was going to do what he said. He told me, "This is our life now." I don't know if my heart was so broken that I didn't care, or if I had given up the dream of a great life with a loving, honest husband, but I decided to do whatever he asked of me.

We kept working hard and bought the house we live in now. It's a much bigger house, in a beautiful neighborhood, and we told each other that we would live there until we retired, or even longer. I continued to work at my nail salon, and he started a landscaping business. I knew that I felt differently toward him, but life was good, and we seemed to be getting along very well. Things were going smoothly, and I was happy again.

But one day, about ten years ago, I discovered that my husband was seeing another woman. I found out from my neighbors that he was having an affair. I worked hard every day, and one of my neighbors told me that when I left the house, my husband would bring another woman home. I was devastated. I couldn't believe that for all those years, it only looked on the outside like true love. I discovered that it was not. I don't know why he did that; I don't understand any of that, but for right now I just have to accept these things. That's just the way it is. I had and have the right to break up with this strange new husband, but I cannot. For some reason I was to stay beside him and keep our family together. I did not want my son to be without his parents, like I was. So I told myself that no matter what, I was still strong enough to resist and see my son grow up over time. I would sacrifice my life to live for my son, even though the love between husband and wife had been betrayed.

CHAPTER 7

So I live like a body without a soul.

The hardest part is that he doesn't get along with my son. He always gives me a hard time, always tells me that I spoil my son. He sees the faith that I have in my son, and he gives me a very hard time about it. Maybe he is jealous of his own son; I don't know. Maybe he is jealous that I get along so well with Anthony. I don't think that I will ever be able to figure out what is going on with him.

My son went off to college, and I was so proud of him. He was able to go to school and get the education that I wanted so desperately. But when my son would come home, my husband would speak very badly to him. He would argue and complain at him, so much so that my son would not want to come home. I have no idea why my husband did that to him. Whenever I talk he just yells back. He looks at me like I am a monster. He does that to my son too, and my heart just keeps getting more broken.

One day I couldn't take it and just had to get out of the house. I decided to go to the tax office at the school district and pay the house taxes. I saw a lady cleaning the building and asked her how she got her job. She told me that I had go to another place to fill out an application for a job, and she knew that they really needed people to work. She gave me the address, but since I can't read, I asked her where it was. She told me many landmarks around where the building was, but when I drove around the place that I thought she meant, I couldn't find it. I went back to the tax office to talk to the lady again, but she wasn't there. It took four times, but I finally found the place, and got the application. I took it home, and my neighbor that is always helping me helped me to fill it out. Right after that they called for an interview. They told me that I would have to come back after they talked to some more people. I just told him that I wanted the job, and that I really didn't want to come back. They gave me the job right then and there.

So I worked at a school doing custodial work. One day I came home from work, and my husband was home. He was very angry with me, or maybe it was at someone else; I do not know what set him off. I had barely spoken to him, but he just kept yelling at me. He was so angry that he punched me in my ribs hard enough to bruise me. I was in a lot of pain the next day. While I was at work, I bent over to get something from the floor, and I winced at the pain in my side. My supervisor saw this and asked me what happened. I told him that I had accidentally walked into a door, that the doorknob had hit me in my ribs. I told the same thing to my son when he could tell that I was having trouble walking and was in pain. No matter how much I don't respect my husband, or sometimes don't like him, I don't want Anthony to know that part about his father.

One very cold day in January, I came home from work, and Tony called me over to him so that we could talk. He told me that he wanted to leave me. He said that he was just going to leave, that he couldn't stand being here anymore, and that I could have the house. He just wanted out. Then I found out that he had started gambling, and he was losing all our money. I couldn't believe it. I was sp upset. My son was home from school and found out about everything. Anthony was so upset, confused, and angry that he decided to quit school and not go back. Anthony just kept asking me why his father did things like this to us. All I could say to my son was that I didn't know why he did this, and to try to just forget about it. I told him that he needed to keep going further, keep the faith in God, and everything would be fine.

It's just difficult, because every time I say anything, he just makes this sound like he is breathing hard and very mad. I just keep talking softly and walk away. Sometimes I can't believe that I have been married for almost thirty years. It just seems sad that for all these years, I haven't known why he does things, and I have no idea what he does behind my back. It is very hard for me. But I am happy right now, because my son is staying with me, and he is going back to school. I just keep talking to him, and I let him talk about how he is feeling inside. I just keep listening to him, and I know that he talked it out and fixed himself. I am very proud of him. During the last year of college, the relationship between my son and my husband was so bad that Anthony had a really hard time at school. He had trouble concentrating and trying to keep focused. He had been in college three and a half years, was almost done, and then just dropped out. That really hurt me at the time. I begged my husband to just talk to his son, and he would just reply, "He's the one who doesn't do anything," and leave it at that. I thought that if Tony were nicer to my son, then he would go back to school. Tony never would even try to talk to him like a man. He just treated him like a burden, not a son.

My son worked very hard, and I am very proud of him. I love my son. It's funny—he is about six feet two, and I am only four feet eight. He is a very tall boy. I love him very much. I want him to be successful; I want him to love his job. I want him to love what he does for work every day. My husband told me one day that I spoil him too much and then told me the next day that he has to buy him a car. I just cringe inside, because I know that he will just fight about it later with Anthony.

Tony has walked on my heart for the last ten years. He thinks that he is so cool, that he can have any woman. He has spent so much money on women, playing the big man, but now he is broke. Most days I have no idea what he does, what he wants to do, but I do know that my heart is strong. He comes home sometimes; he stays away for days other times. When he gets mad at someone or something, he will come home and take it out on me. He yells at me constantly and tells me how stupid I am. That is the part that really hurts. He tries to make fun of me by saying things like, "Do I have to listen to you? No, I don't, because you don't know anything." It hurts so much when he calls me stupid. He tells me things like, "I would leave you, but you don't know how to read or write." That is just so hurtful to me. I know that I was never able to have a real education, but I don't feel like I am stupid. Education does make you smarter, but you have to have a brain to work with in the first place. I think if my brain had gotten a chance to learn everything it could, I would be just like everyone else.

I just put my hand on my forehead exasperated, and asked my husband what I did wrong. What did I ever do to him to deserve this kind of treatment? He just lowered his head and told me that I did nothing wrong, and that when he dies he will bring his problems all to death with him.

CHAPTER 8

*My heart is on my future. I am strong. I don't want
to die and leave my son, like my parents left me. I ask
God for help. I go to church, I go to the temple, and
I pray for God to help me; I pray for Buddha to help
me. When I look at myself in the mirror, sometimes I
am Helen; sometimes I am Helen, and sometimes I am
Tang. I'm just a little girl, little girl. That's just how
it is, and I stay strong. That's why I want to write this
book. I want to say, look at what matters; it doesn't
matter, just walk away, and turn around and do
the right thing. You never, never stop learning until
the day you close your eyes. Do what I do. If I think
what I am doing is wrong, I just ask God for help.*

My life has been very sad, but I know that God will help
me, so I remain very strong. God helps me cope and to look
forward to having a future someday. I believe that he will help
me with whatever I want in my life. On the outside everybody

thinks that I am so happy. I always laugh and talk, but on the inside I am very hurt. I am hurt from losing my parents and family early in life. I am hurt from having an adoptive mother that didn't care about me, and I hurt from my husband. But I will always continue to stay strong, and God will continue to be on my side. I just keep doing the things I have to do. I just keep working, and I always try to keep a positive attitude. I know that God is helping me to stay strong.

My adoptive mother is seventy-three years old now and constantly asks me to come to her house to help her when I don't have to work. I realize now that she is still desperate to control me. She does not live very close to me, and I do not like going to her house. But she is old, and I feel like sometimes I am the only one that is there to help her. Why I feel obligated to help her is beyond me. One day she begged me to come over and make her some food. She told me that she was sick and could not feed herself or my father. Since he doesn't know how to cook, I felt sorry for her and went to the store to get some groceries and then drove all the way to her house. When I got there, she seemed fine. She was not acting like she was sick at all. My father was not home, and I asked where he was. She told me he was working. I got pretty upset at myself for letting her trick me, but I thought since I was there, I would smile, make the meal for her, and then go home. When I told her that I was finished with the dinner, she told me that she would not eat it. I was stunned. She told me that she did not want to eat what I had prepared, so she was going to call my father so he could bring better food home with him. After that I usually tried to get out of going to her house to help her, by saying I had to work or that I already had something to do on my day off. She still called all the time, but I would just get out of going somehow.

Then came a day when I felt guilty for not going for so long, and I agreed to drive to her house to help her with something. While I was there, I decided to take the opportunity to ask her why she hadn't let me learn, why she hadn't let me go to school and have a normal life. She got mad and said, "Now that I am old, you want to start trouble with me? After all these years, you now want to say something to me?" I told her that I just had questions that I needed her to answer. All I wanted to know is why she wouldn't let me go to school. Why did her other children grow and thrive, while she insisted that I stay home and do the housework? She told me that at that time she was just young and didn't know what she was doing. She didn't want to talk about it. She just turned her back on me and refused to talk. She wouldn't even listen to me anymore. Maybe because she is old she doesn't want to talk about it.

I often wonder if she ever feels guilty for the way she treated me. I usually try to see the good in her, try to believe that she just didn't know better, but then I think that maybe she just never really learned how to love anyone. She probably doesn't love herself, so it was impossible for her to love me.

When we are together now, she pretends that she likes me and acts nice to me in front of my brothers and sisters. She acts like she loves me just as much as the others, but I know the truth. I get along with everybody, except my mom. She has always given me a very hard time. She used me all of the time. I had to take care of her kids, and her home. When I worked I always had to give her all my money. She acts so sweet to me when others are around, but then she will do something behind their backs, to make sure that I know she still feels the same about me. It has been such a hard way to live. I just always wonder why she is like this. Why does she act this way? What did I ever do to her to make her feel and act this way toward me? I'm beginning to think that I will never have an answer to my questions.

CHAPTER 9

I am thankful that my adoptive parents gave me food, and a life, but my mom would not let me go to school. I still want to learn how to read and write very badly. I cannot read or write, but I work seven days a week and always try to stay strong. I want to be able to read and write in Vietnamese too. I get very sad when I think about my mom and my dad and how they went away. They left me, and they are gone. I want to tell my story, but it is so, so sad. I didn't tell my husband my story. I didn't tell my son my story.

My whole adoptive family lives in America now. They live in different places, but they keep in contact with me and make me feel like I am a part of the family. I do respect my mom and dad very much, even though all of these problems have gone on for many years. I asked my adoptive dad one day if he could tell me what I did wrong. I asked him to tell me why he thought that I was not allowed to go to school. I asked him why he and my mother treated me differently. His only response was that he just didn't know. He would not tell me, or if he did know why, he wouldn't say. Now my father is gone; he died December 4, 2011, when he was eighty-four. My mom waited until December 10 to put him in his casket and then buried him on December 11. Those dates are my son's birthday and my birthday. Sometimes I wonder why she did that, whether it was supposed to mean something. I know my mom knew that my dad was kind to me at times. He tried to make things better for me, in little ways, but it was always kept a secret. He didn't want her to know that he felt bad for me. I always appreciated that about him. I know that he just did the best he could with the circumstances that surrounded us.

I guess I will never know why she did some of the things that she did. Maybe it is better for me not to know. Maybe even she doesn't know. I wonder about that sometimes. I wonder about a lot of things but then just try to think that God has a plan for me, and that plan will go on no matter what. I trust in that.

CHAPTER 10

I live a happy life now because my son is close to me. He lives nearby, and we talk all the time. We are very close, and sometimes that makes me know that I can survive this. I think sometimes I just live day by day. I work hard and keep going, no matter what. If my son needs me, I will be there for him. I know that I have to stay strong for him. I have to stay strong to protect him. I worry all the time, but in my heart I know God will help me. I know that Buddha will help me. Most days I know that everything will be all right in the end.

For a while I had a little store at the flea market where I sold kitchen tools. I worked at the school full-time, and then each weekend I would go on Saturday and Sunday to sell kitchen items in my little store. It was a very good living at first, but then sales started dwindling more and more. After a few years I decided to stop trying to sell items at the flea market. I wasn't selling as much as I had before, and I was hardly making any money. It wasn't worth the time it took to keep going there. Sometimes I don't know how to keep these problems at bay. I do have to stay strong so I can protect my child. That is so important to me.

Everything in my life has been so painful, except for my son. I think that some of the worrying and stress that I have had to endure has caused me to have high blood pressure and diabetes. I do not have medical insurance to help me with medication, but I just keep going along and try to do the right things. I just live day by day, month after month, year after year. I never know what is going to happen next, but I do believe that God will continue to help me along the way. He always has. I continue to do what I think is right and to do my own thing. I want the world to know that I am proud of myself, because through all of this, I have stayed strong.

CHAPTER 11

I am strong and would say to anyone that you should keep working and going, and God will make it right. This has worked for me, and it will work for you. Thank God, ask him to bless you when things get deeper and deeper, but it will be all right. Don't turn around. Keep walking. Just keep doing what you have to do.

After we had lived in our house for fourteen years, the water pipes broke. There was water all over the house. I called my husband to come home and help me, but he just told me to go to a neighbor's house and tell them what happened, so they could help. I went to a neighbor's house, but they told me that they couldn't help me. My husband finally came home, and we went to anther neighbor to help us with getting the furniture out. She was extremely helpful; she helped us move furniture and sweep the water out of the house. She also assisted us by calling the insurance company. The insurance company said they would pay for the repairs, but the repairs would take three to four months. I liked the wood on my floors, so I went to the store to get some wood that was the same. They didn't have the same kind, so my husband told me that he was going to go to the hardware store to find some new materials for our floors. He called me to tell me that he found what he liked, and that I should come over to see if I liked this new flooring.

I told him I would come to look, and I walked around the flooring section to see what they had, and if there was anything I liked. He finally showed me the flooring that he had picked out, but I told him that the design was too busy, because we have so much other color in the house. I just suggested that we get something that was more one color, something neutral that would go with everything. I could tell that that made him extremely upset, and he started yelling at me to get out of the store. He told me to leave, and that I didn't know what I was talking about. The guy that was helping us just stared at him in embarrassment. I told Tony that he shouldn't yell at me, because he had asked for my opinion, and I was just telling him what I thought. I told him that since the house belonged to both of us, we should be able to discuss things like this. He was so mad, he just kept yelling at me. He looked embarrassed too, and I think he knew he was wrong for doing that, but he just kept yelling. He wouldn't stop, so I just left the store and drove to work.

CHAPTER 12

He pokes a thousand holes into my heart.

Soon after the pipes broke, my mother called me to say that my father had died. I called my husband to tell him, and to tell him when the funeral was. He told me that he couldn't, because he had to watch them put the new floor in. My son was in college, and I didn't want him to have to fly home, so I told him to stay in school. Tony refused to go to the funeral with me, so I went by myself.

When I got back from the funeral, I walked around and saw that the floor wasn't even, and that it was too busy, with just too many colors. When I swept the floor, the dirt caught in the grooves, and I would have to bend over and pick it up. I wanted to tell Tony what was happening with the new floor and ask him to get the people to redo the floor the right away. I just made some small talk and walked away. I knew that he would blow up if I said anything more about the floor. Now the floor is done; it is very colorful and has too much going on with it. It's obvious that he doesn't like it, but he says that he likes it so that I won't be right. He told me that he would agree to redo the floor but then changed his mind and says to me that he does like it. It doesn't matter. When I talk he does not listen to me anyway.

CHAPTER 13

Very tough. Very hard. Happy today, and sad next
day. And sad more than happy. Everything is so many
different ways. All I know to say good, good, good,
good. I'm happy, happy, happy until I been married
for twenty-eight years. Everything is going fine,
everything is going good; someday we'll be happy.

In the years after I found out my husband was having affairs, he never gave me any money. I had to work to support myself. I met a guy named Paul who sold kitchen tools like blenders, meat choppers, and pots and pans that he got from Macy's. He told me that he sold these kitchen items at a flea market, and that he made lots of money. I talked to him and asked if I could follow him to the flea market so that I could see his store and how he does it. I went home that night and told my husband that I was going to meet with a guy the next day and explained what I was doing. To my surprise, my husband said he was going to go with me. I laughed; was he jealous?

So instead of arguing with him, I just told him when I was going, and when he needed to be ready.

I bought about two hundred dollars worth of merchandise and worked very hard at selling everything so that I could afford to buy more items to sell. I worked every weekend and eventually had over $35,000 worth of merchandise. I was so proud of myself! The hard part was trying to deal with people that would come to my store and expect me to sell expensive items for a few dollars. They would tell me that I should be happy that they were even offering me money at all, since I was working in a flea market. I guess because I speak with an accent, some people assume that I don't know what I am doing. They have no respect for what I have accomplished, and how much work I have put into this store.

During this time I also worked as a custodian for a school district, and I worked at many different schools. So finally I felt like I did it, I was making a living all by myself. I was very proud of myself, and what I had accomplished for my son and myself.

But my home life had gotten worse. My husband had a very bad temper, and I had to walk on eggshells and find the right words to speak to him. If I said the wrong thing, he would yell very loudly, so much so that Anthony asked me one day if his dad had never really learned how to talk, whether he just learned how to yell. I told him that we will never win, so the best thing to do is to listen to him and try not to go deaf. After that, whenever Tony would yell at me, I would just walk by and say, "I'm not deaf!"

I thought it was funny, but then he would get mad and break the TV or my dryer, so I just stopped saying things like that and was careful with my words. The amusement it brought me was not worth the damage it caused.

One time I didn't feel safe in my house, so I told my neighbor to watch out for me. I told her that if anything happened to me, then my husband probably did it. He constantly has women over, and he thinks he is so smart, and that I don't know, but of course I do.

My brothers and my sisters have a good life, and I guess I do too. If I hear a sad story, or see something on the news, I always want to tell those people to not give up, to be strong and stay strong. It has been about fifty-three years that I have been going through this difficult life. But I still say that you must stay strong. I like to tell people to go to church, just sit and relax and talk to God. I tell them that if they do this, their lives will still be hard, but it will get you through this. I also believe that you shouldn't feel bad for yourself. I know sometimes, I think, *Oh well, I can't do this anymore.* Then I realize that I just have to keep going; I have to keep being happy and keep God around me. I just have to do this, do it for my life, and do it for my son.

I think about being a little girl, about being a wife and mother, and how hard everything has been for me. It's not easy, but I just talk to myself and say that God is with me. Sometimes I talk to myself, or sometimes I like to sing to myself, and people probably think I am crazy. I don't care, because I just keep going on and do what is right. That keeps me strong and helps me to know that I can be strong in everything I do.

Day after day, month after month, year after year, my husband fights with me. He does things that he knows are wrong, and I just watch to see how far he goes. I just wait to see what happens. I just keep quiet. I just wait and watch him dig a hole for himself. He just keeps filling in the hole, and then he digs it again. Every time he digs a hole, it hurts me to watch it, but there is nothing I can do. He treats me like a little ant; I believe that he thinks that one day he can just squish me.

CHAPTER 14

I want to be a United States citizen. I have taken the test three times, but I cannot read or write, so I cannot pass. I want to learn to read and write so bad. I have gone to night school to try to learn how to read and write. It is going very slowly, but I keep trying.

When I get sad about my life, I just think about happy times. When Ken got old enough, he knew I didn't know how to drive. He knew that if he left it up to my mother, she would never teach me. I think he understood more than anyone else about all of this, about my situation in that family. He would always teach me things and do things for me. I had no idea how to do anything other than what needed to be done around the house. He tried to help me, and I will always be thankful to him for that.

Even though I do have some good memories of growing up, most are not very pleasant. I remember one time that my little sister and I were fighting. We were really just playing around, and it went too far. I wanted to try to turn the situation around and so decided to start a peek-a-boo game with her to make her laugh. But when I said "Boo!" it was too loud, and it scared her. She was little and she started to cry. My mom came in to see why she was crying, and my sister told my mom that I had scared her. She was too little to know that it was just a game. So my mom hit me for that. She hit me very hard, and I remember how much that hurt. I got hit, but I also learned.

One time my brother Ken was skipping school. He was only about eleven or twelve years old at the time. He would get dropped off at the front of the school, but then he would leave and not go in. He did this for about a month. The school called home to see what was wrong with Ken. They told my dad that Ken hadn't been to school for a month. When my father told my mother about this, my mother got very angry and tied my brother to a pole in the backyard. She wouldn't let him eat or drink. My sisters and I gave him some food. We gave him some water. I remember that we had to keep the bugs and ants off his feet. There were bugs everywhere, flying around him. His hands were tied in the back, so he couldn't get the bugs off him, so we did it for him. He stayed there the rest of that day and then all night. When he was freed, he thanked us for helping him and told me that there were four rules in the house that I should memorize. They were:

1. Don't talk back to Mom.
2. Don't get mad at what happens.
3. Just always be happy.
4. It doesn't matter what happens; Mom doesn't get along with her other daughters either.

It was then that I realized that it really didn't matter what I said or did; it mattered only that I keep the peace within myself, always do what is right, and stay strong with God on my side.

CHAPTER 15

I can't believe it. Unbelievable—my adoptive mother—
when I think back on all the things she did to me.
But it's my life. It is really hard, and how did I find
the way to be strong, find the way to keep walking,
find the way to be strong to live? But I just look up,
and even though my life isn't easy, I thank God.

My brother Ken is a pharmacist. My sister Amy went to college for two years and then got married and didn't want to go back to school. I still get along with them very well and talk with them often. My mom will call me, sometimes in the middle of the night, to help her with things. When I ask her to call Amy or Ken, she tells me that they are important and far too busy for such things. She tells me that they work hard, and that I am the only one that has time to run errands for her. It's so funny to me, because I actually work way more hours than they do, and probably don't make nearly as much money. She still thinks that I need to cook for her or her family.

Just recently when she called me to have me do something for her, I told her that I am sorry, but I am busy and cannot do those kinds of favors for her anymore. She got very angry with me. It seems like we get along worse now. On the rare occasions that we do talk now, when I say anything to her, she doesn't like it. She will just try to convince me to come over to her house, because she wants me to cook, to clean, and to take care of her like when I was little. But I have a family now that I need to take care of, and I can't do that.

More than that, I don't want to do things for her anymore. I have my own life now. I'm not like I was before; I am much stronger. I want to tell her that sometimes I would like to relax and not run around town on my day off, but she just keeps yelling that she needs me to do things, and there is nobody else to help her. I don't know what to say to that, I can't make her understand, so I usually just don't answer her calls. Because of that, she says that I don't even try to get along with her. When I do break down and go over to her house, I tell her that I can help her with only one thing. She always tells me that she needs me to do three. If I say I will do two things, she says she needs ten things. I honestly can't believe that she still expects me to cook for her, to cook for her family. I just try to leave her alone. I think it's very sad that she still wants me to do all of these things, but I tell myself that it is her problem now. I just can't do it anymore.

CHAPTER 16

I told my sister Amy one time, "I wish somebody could write a book about this, about my life." She just said, "Oh no. You don't need to." I told her that I could tell her the story, and she could write the book, but she said she didn't know how to do that. I can't say anything; I can't do anything. But then God helped me to find Ms. Leslie.

On the outside, to everyone else, it looks like I have a very happy life. My husband invites people to our house, usually some workers or friends, and I always cook and act like nothing is wrong. It looks to everyone on the outside that I have a very beautiful home, a loving husband, and a lot to be happy about. But as soon as people leave to go home, my husband will try to start a fight and tell me things that I did wrong. Or maybe he will pick on something that I said.

I have a couple neighbors that are sweet and tell me that they will look after me. They watch my house and listen to hear if anything is wrong. My husband always talks to others about what a great wife he has, what a great cook I am, but then he comes home and is very unhappy. He usually comes home very late, and sometimes I pretend I am asleep. He gets in bed and just rolls around in bed and sighs. He has much pain inside that is there every day. I would like to help him, but I just have to take it all in and swallow it up inside. Sometimes I just wonder if everybody has to take it like this.

One time my son and I were eating, and my husband came home early and asked if there was any food left over. I had plenty of food, and he asked if he could have some rice. Everything was going very well, so I told him about the registration stickers that were due on the boat. He got very mad and started yelling about it. He then told me that the rice was too salty, when he had just been eating it a minute before and obviously liked it. Maybe he didn't have money for the boat, so he decided to take it out on me. I just stood there and took it, and I didn't say any more. He kept yelling about the rice.

Now that my son is here, I am not really that scared anymore that something will happen to me. I don't think that he will hit me when Anthony is living here at the house. If he tried, I think my son would keep him from doing anything to me.

I constantly ask him why he is so angry with me. I ask him what I did to make him yell at me so much. I try so hard to be sweet to him, but it doesn't work. He just tells me that I have done nothing wrong. He says that whatever is wrong in his life, he has brought on himself.

So I just stay quiet and go about my business. I just pray that I stay strong, and I tell myself that he is only a human, not God. Sometimes I just stare into space and feel like I am seven years old and living with my adoptive parents again. It feels like when my mother would beat me, and she would not want or know how to be a mother to me. She will always be a mother for her other children, but she will never be a mother to me. Sometimes I just have to say to myself that it is amazing that I lived with her for almost twenty years, and I still can't believe or understand what happened.

Chapter 17

Today is April 30, and I am being a lazy cook today. I am going to order some fried rice. Every day is a busy day; always my mind is wondering what is going to happen next. Today I just had to walk away from my husband; he was angry.

I remember one time in 1984, after we got married, I went to my husband's home. I met his family and could tell that he was a daddy's boy. He fought with his mother every day, but I really liked her. I invited her to come to the United States with me, and she was so happy that I did that. She opened up to me and asked about my upbringing. I told her a little about the life that I had so far. I told her that I had gone through a lot in my life and told her about my adoptive mother. She told me that she'd had to deal with a lot going on in her life too. She told me that she respected her husband greatly and treated him like a king, but in turn he treated her like a maid. She told me that he hit her very hard and did it often. I told her lots of people come to the United States and go through the court system to get a divorce. But then I felt bad for saying that. I realized that this was her life, and I really had no idea what was going on with her. I decided to stay out of her business and let her ask me for help if she wanted it. I think she was scared, and I knew how that felt. I just told her that I would help her at any time and decided to leave it at that. When I got back home, I made a list of things that I was grateful for. I made that list to remind me that I have more than I think, and I can be happy.

Sometimes when I think about how bad my childhood was, and how bad my marriage is, I have to think about my son. He will be twenty-eight soon, and I can't believe that sometimes. Time passes by so quickly. Every day I use him as a symbol to tell me that everything will be fine. I see him and remember that I have to stay strong in my body. I see him and remember that I have to stay strong in my mind. I wish that people could hear my story and know that if they have a life like mine, they need to find something that matters to them, and they will find strength in that. They need to stay strong, and on a good path. They need to listen to their hearts and do the things that they know are right, even when everything around them is wrong.

I teach my son that if he does something wrong, he needs to say he's sorry. I never tell him that he has to do everything my way, but he does need to do things the right way. I tell him to keep his heart open, and also his eyes. You can have a thousand hands; you can have a thousand eyes. Some people take that power and do the wrong thing. Some people just use the ability to look the other way as a tool, as a weapon to hurt. My husband has a thousand eyes. My adoptive mother has a thousand eyes. They look everywhere with those eyes except where they should be looking. I hope that when they finally close their eyes, they will find peace.

My husband says bad things to me, and it hurts. My mother says horrible things to me, and that hurts just as much. I had the thought one time that life is like a hurricane. The wind comes up, the rain comes up, but it has to stop at some point. It does a lot of damage to everything along its path, but it always stops. I just have to wait for it to stop. Life is just like a hurricane.

Most days I feel like I still love my husband, even when he is mean. He is just so mad all the time. He is mad at me, he is mad at his son, he is mad at his employees. One day I asked him if he needed to go to a hospital. He gave me such a strange look, because there was nothing wrong with him. He asked me why he would want to go to the hospital, and I told him I think that his brain is not working right. A brain can't be healthy and treat someone else like he treats me. He just laughed at me, and then got mad again. I don't understand him at all. I think he is selfish. I know he has a hot temper, but I never know what to say to him. I know that I shouldn't have said that to him, but I get so tired of the same routine. I decided to walk away. I just go my way, and he just goes his.

In January of 2012, he told me that he was going to leave me. I was very upset and tried to talk to him rationally. I told him, "If you want me to say I'm sorry, then I will say I'm sorry. I am sorry for whatever makes you so unhappy. If it is me, then I will do something about it." He told me that I don't have anything to be sorry for. He just wants to leave. I feel like I always do what he wants me to do. I cook for his friends—sometimes thirty or more people at time. Everybody laughs and eats and drinks, and I look like I am the happiest person in the world. No one would guess that I am miserable all the time.

Now, after he's told me he wants to leave, I do a lot of things by myself. If I am hungry, I cook something for myself, and I do not wait for him to eat with me anymore. He told me that his son should always do the right thing. He doesn't realize that he is a very poor role model of a husband and father. He thinks that if he tells us something, then that is how it is. He doesn't realize that when we see his actions, we respond according to those, and not just to what he is telling us. So far Anthony is a very good boy, and I hope he stays that way. I hope that he remembers how his father treated me and knows that he never wants to be that way with a wife, that he never wants to be that way with his children. Hopefully, he will see that if I stay strong, he can get through anything. If I keep going to church, if I keep doing the things that I know are right, he will see that example too and not go the other way.

For a while I had a dog, and I talked to him like a person. He seemed to understand me and was always so happy when he saw me. He was a little Chihuahua, and I named him Castle. I loved him very much. Castle kept me company every day. I liked having something around that loved me and seemed to be happy just to be by my side. One day Castle wasn't feeling well, so I watched him very carefully. I took him to the vet, and they told me that he had cancer. I watched him day by day, and he just got worse. Eventually, Castle was so sick that he was unable to walk very far. A few times he had an accident in the house, and my husband would get very angry and hit him. I couldn't believe it. I had to put a diaper on him so he wouldn't go to the bathroom in the house and upset my husband. How can you hit a little dog that is sick? My Castle finally died; he just went to sleep. He didn't make any noise, he didn't cry, he just died. I was very sad, but in my heart I knew that Castle felt very loved by me and knew that I always took good care of him. It still makes me sad to think about him.

My husband doesn't care anymore. He still has a lot of family at home. His mother is fine, but his brothers and sister aren't. He doesn't speak to them. I think he is just a broken man. I asked him why he doesn't have a relationship with his family, and he just yelled at me. He says things to me to make me feel stupid, but he doesn't have any idea how strong I am. I can't say that it doesn't hurt, but it won't kill me. When things like this happen, I don't say anything more to him; I just walk away. I wonder sometimes what he really thinks about me. I wonder if he sees how strong I am and then tries harder to break me. Most of the time he acts like my son and I are nothing to him, and everything else in the world matters. Sometimes he looks at me like I am a monster. I just really wonder what he is thinking. When he does talk, he can't say anything to me without being mean. Sometimes he doesn't come home at night, and I will ask him where he has been. He will tell me that he was in the warehouse, because he was too tired to come home. I just say okay or something simple like that. He thinks that I am clueless to what is going on, but I am not clueless; I know. Things like this have been going on for fifteen years.

He came to me a little while ago and told me that he had talked to a lawyer about getting a divorce. He told me the lawyer said he would have to wait six months to divorce me. So I waited for six months, but nothing happened. I have no idea what is going on with that. I just listen to what he says, and I let it go in one ear and out the other. I basically ignore everything he says now and act like I care, act like I am listening. Every time he talks to me, I listen to him and act like I respect him. Sometimes when he is being nice, I will try to talk to him, but he just ignores me. He won't listen to one single thing I say.

One day he told me to shut up and stop talking. I thought he wanted to say something to me, but he kept quiet. I finally said, "Can I ask you something?" All he said was, "Why?" and told me to shut up again. I asked him to think about what he was doing. I had to listen to him, but he did not have to listen to me. I asked him if he thought that was fair, and he didn't answer me at all.

When he is home, he mostly just sits downstairs, so I go upstairs to my room. I know that when he is out, he gambles and drinks, and he tries to get the girls. He is so reckless with our money; he spends it all and doesn't think about what we need for the house. He also has to send money home to his family. I don't mind when he sends his mother some money, but he also has to send it to his twelve brothers and sisters, because his mom tells him he has to. There are so many in his family, and they just wait around for him to supply the money to them. I know that this is his family, but when he got married and had a baby, we became his family too. He should take care of this family that he made too.

From six years old to now—and I am fifty-three—I have kept this entire story inside of me. I never feel like I can talk this out with anybody, because I am afraid someone will say something. So I just kept it in for a long, long time. One day I may have a sad day. The next day may be a happy day. One day might be a headache day. Is that the way we are supposed to live? Is this my future? Some days I want to cry out, very loud. Some days I just want to get away from the headaches, the crazy life. I cannot do all of the things that I want to do, because I cannot read or write. I can do labor, I can work hard, but I feel like then everybody just takes from me. But I won't give up. I will never give up. So sometimes I have to look like I know how to write to other people. I laugh, I smile, I ask people how they are doing. They will say they have a pain, or that they are tired, and I still just tell them that I am doing great. God has finally sent me a friend that will help me. God knows that my story will help other people stay strong. Stay positive. Please, God, help me to stay strong.

CHAPTER 18

*I don't know what to say sometimes when I turn
this machine on and talk, but then things just
come out. It's funny sometimes. It's very funny.
Sometimes I get to where I can't talk anymore.*

I like to walk to the big Chinese apple tree. The tree has so
many blooms, and it makes me happy. I watch the tree and
beg it to give me bigger blooms. I like it when the tree gives
me bigger blooms. I stare at the tree and try to think of happy
things, of happier times. It works until I think about how long
I have been married. Everything changes, everything is going
well in my life. Then one day it all changes, and it all goes in
a downward spiral. Oh, apple tree, help me see the good in
everything, like I see in you.

Lately I feel like I really need to learn how to read and write.
I want people to be able to understand me when I talk. Some
people tell me that I speak English very well, but then they

squint and turn their ears toward me. I know that they are having a difficult time understanding what I am saying. They have no idea that all this stuff has happened to me, and I just go on. I just bite my tongue.

My son is home now, and he helps me with the house. Every time I look at my house, I know that I love my house and do not want to leave it. There are many things around my home that I love. So what am I supposed to do? Sometimes I can tell that my son is so unhappy living here. He says that he doesn't understand how I put up with his daddy. I told him that he shouldn't worry about all of that now, and that when he is older, he will understand. He will know how to deal with his dad someday. There are so many times that you have to make a choice. There are so many times when you don't have to, but you just keep working hard and do what you know is right. That's all I can tell him. Then I show him that I am strong. I laugh and I do things without anybody knowing what is really inside of me.

I don't have anybody in my family to really help me. I don't understand why my husband has such hate in his heart. I wish he would wake up and smell the coffee. He has a beautiful son, and a wife that never gives him any trouble. Just recently a man came to me and said, "You are so beautiful; I think you have a beautiful body. You are so friendly and so nice." I immediately thought, "You need to take care of your family. You should not be saying that to me," but I didn't say anything to him. I just smiled and walked away.

CHAPTER 19

Happy today, sad the next day. But I am sad more than happy. Everything is so many different ways. You think that this is good to talk? I walk around with a lot of things on my mind. All I know to say is good, good, good.

It's funny, but my husband does things that he should not do, and then he gets in trouble. But even when he is in really big trouble, I never tell him that I am going to kick him out. I don't call him stupid for making a bad choice. I don't tell him that he has no idea what he is doing: *You think you are a big man? You think you are the big boss? You should just turn yourself around and do the right thing.* He is just like my mom. She says bad things, she does bad things, and then bad things happen to her.

It's just not right to say bad things. When my mom does this, her body starts to give her trouble; it is trying to tell her that she should stop doing these things. I know that if she stopped, she would feel like a new person. Her body reacts to her actions, and then she calls me to help her because she is in pain. If I don't go to her immediately, she complains again that I don't do things for her. That's what happens every time. I have told her a million times that she shouldn't act sweet in front of people and then say mean things to me. It is bad for her. I know that when everything is gone from her body, she might say, "Oh, I am so sorry—I did so many things wrong," but she doesn't realize that it doesn't work like that. I can never get through to her that it just doesn't work like that.

CHAPTER 20

---

*You pass the day, the month, you pass the year, and
I am still here. I just say "Thank God," and I make
a list. I made a list of things to make me happy.*

Sometimes I think, "Oh my God, I can't keep these things
in my mind," and then I really don't feel like doing anything.
My husband brings friends home, and he wants me to cook a
big meal for them. I do it, but then I get tired of cooking, so
I just won't cook for a while. I don't cook for him, and I don't
cook for me. I clean my house, but his friends mess it up, so
I leave it. I want my husband to say thank you for cooking
and cleaning, but he won't. He won't help either. So I refuse
to cook or clean, but then I look around, and I can't stand
that my house is so dirty, so I have to clean. It's unbelievable.
I just bite my tongue.

My husband has had many different girlfriends. I just don't
understand it. I don't know why he thinks that is so fun. I

found out that a woman that my husband is in love with has eight children. I saw the woman in the grocery store when I was with a friend. The woman came up to my friend and started talking to her. She told my friend that she wanted to know about me. She asked my friend a lot of questions about me, and my friend asked her a lot of questions. She said that her eight children are all grown, and not living with her anymore. I went home that night and told my husband everything that had happened in the grocery store. I was so upset and asked him if all of this was fun for him. He said that the only fun he has is gambling. I asked him if he thought that the reason he had so many women was because of a cultural thing, like something in the Vietnamese culture. He said he didn't know. I told him that I know that in many countries, married men have girlfriends, but when the wives find out, then they get a divorce. He told me that if I tried to get a divorce, he would kill me. He told me that he didn't think I was the type of person to just go out and get a divorce. He said that I would never do that to him. He said that a divorce would never be an option for me. I told him that I might just go get a divorce if I felt like it.

I asked him why he thought it was okay for him to go out with other women all the time and expect me to just sit and take it. I wonder sometimes why I can't just go out and do whatever I want, go and find someone to love me, but he probably knows that I really won't. I know that I really would never do that. So many of his friends like me enough to call and tell me everything that he does behind my back. I tell them that I don't believe them, because if they thought that I did, they would just talk and talk all the time about it. They will just keep going on and on about this and that, and everything that he does.

Believe it or not, sometimes women flirt with my husband right in front of me. They can see a ring on my finger and should assume that I am his wife. He flirts back with them, and it hurts me very much. I'm standing right there and have to watch it all. I know my husband is still handsome, and they must think that he is a really good man, but how can he be a good man and do that to me? They just want him to spend money on them, that's all. I don't think they want a husband; they just want his things. I see women out in front of our house sometimes, and I just think to myself that they are dirty, and I go to my room and try to not to think about it.

When I first found out about all these women, I was really sad. I walked around hurt all of the time, and it showed. I didn't like how I felt, and I didn't like how I acted. But now if you looked inside me, looked at my heart, you would see only a rock, a single stone. Whatever my husband says, whatever he does, I still love him, but I am not in love with him. I go to church or the temple, and I just try to pray that someday I will understand.

My friends tell me that even though he is nice to me in front of other people, they know that he does not respect me. They can tell by the things he says when I am not around. They tell me that when he talks about me, it is never very nice. They tell me to wake up and stop living in denial. They ask me what I will do the day he finally leaves and takes everything I have. I just feel sad, and I tell them that I don't know, and that I don't think he will ever do that to me.

One time a friend told me that she was talking to her husband about the fact that I allow my husband to just go out and do whatever he wants. She told him that even though I let my husband do that, she would not allow it. She told him that she would never let her husband do that to her. She told him that she had a gun, and that she would kill him. I really didn't think she would ever do that, so I wasn't worried about it. Then a little while later, I found out that her husband had a girlfriend. I was really shocked, but I didn't say one word to her. She eventually found out from someone else. She was so sad that her husband had a girlfriend that she said she was going to kill herself. I went over there to try to help her, but when I got to her house, I discovered that she had taken a whole bottle of aspirin. Her brother-in-law was living with her, and her son was home that day, so they called 911. She got help in time, but the aspirin did a lot of damage to her stomach and colon. When she eats food now, she can take only small bites and cannot eat very much food at a time. The doctor said that her colon could explode if she eats too much at one time, so she has to eat small portions. When she eats too much, she gets very sick.

After she was feeling better, she called and asked if she could come over to talk to me. She came to my house and shared her story with me. She still did not know that I knew all about her husband, and I did not want her to feel embarrassed, so I just let her talk. She told me the whole story from beginning to end and said that she had made a big mistake. I told her that it was human to make mistakes. Sometimes in life we think that everything is going along very well, and then something happens. I told her to stay strong, and just be glad that her brother-in-law and son were there to help her. Hopefully, she learned a valuable lesson about life and is glad that she was saved.

When I think about people like my friend, I wonder if I should just try to be a good wife, so my husband won't go out with other women. I wonder, *What if I try really hard to be perfect? He will be nice to me, and we can fix what is wrong.* I dream about trying to renew our marriage. So many times

I want to ask Tony if we can start all over again. Then I stop daydreaming and know that I just have to bite my tongue. I have to keep quiet, because I know in my heart that these things will never happen. I just stay busy with work and try to be the best person I can be. I get sad, of course, but then I remember that I am happy with my son, I am happy with my house, and I am happy with myself. I really wouldn't mind if he wanted to start everything over but also think that if he never wanted to do that, then that is fine as well. I just try to do the right thing for myself.

I want to tell people to be strong. I have to listen to what is going on, and I have to do the right thing. You know, if you are walking somewhere and step on a nail, it hurts. If you decide to keep walking on it, you know that it is going to hurt, and you know that you are going to have to take out the nail if you want the pain to stop. If you take out the nail, then it won't hurt anymore. I am very proud of myself, and I am proud that I am very strong. I have a beautiful son; I have a beautiful home and a beautiful life. I can see what is going on, and I have taken the nails out of my feet, and I just keep walking.

Then my husband says to me that he is the man, he is the boss, and that I have to listen to him because he is my husband. Sometimes I just don't know if I can listen to him anymore, because he does things that are difficult for me to understand. But since my son came home from school, things are much easier for me. Since he came home, it helps me a lot just to have him there. I feel happy; I feel like I am doing well. Things are much better now that Anthony is going back to school, because he is home much more. He has a job and should be able to finish school within a year. When everything is relaxed around the house, and my husband is gone, we are like friends, and he just talks and talks. I love that.

I believe that there is still time for me to make a good life. I believe there is still time for me to make an easier life. When I would get hit by my mom, I quickly learned that everything is not easy. If someone hears my story, someone who has a similar life or a life that is very difficult, I want to tell them to please be strong. Please be strong, kind, and patient, and you will have a beautiful life.

One time I saw a show on TV about a homeless couple that had to live in a car. The only thing they had was a van. The woman was pregnant, and she stood on the corner and waited for people to give her money. Her husband didn't eat as much, because he had to save food for her to eat because of the baby. She had a family, but her parents wouldn't accept him, because he was young and did some stupid things and got in trouble with the law. But she was in love and decided to leave her family and live with him, even though he was homeless. And that was it. She made a decision out of love, and at the end of the show, she ended up getting a beautiful house. I think it was because she stayed with love, with the one she gave her heart to. I thought that it was such a beautiful story, and it inspired me.

CHAPTER 21

There is a Vietnamese song. The guy that sings the song, he sings my life. He sings that he lost his mother, and he lost his father, so he is homeless, and there is no one to help.

One time I worked with another Vietnamese lady. She decided to tell me her life story. She told me that she had a lot of boyfriends, but she had a lot of problems too. She was very depressed and felt troubled most of the time. She told me that she had three children with three different fathers. Her boyfriend was in jail, so she had to take care of the kids all by herself. At one point she had nowhere to go, so she brought her children home to live with her mother, but her mother eventually kicked her out. She had three children, and no home, so she walked away and started hitchhiking. Her oldest daughter was fourteen years old, and one day she saw her mom wearing a dress that was very short. She begged her mom to stop doing things that got her in trouble. That little girl must have been so strong. She helped take care of her little brother and sister, didn't have a good role model to help her, and still knew right from wrong. I felt bad for the little girl, because I felt like I had been in that spot. They never had much food to eat, never had much money. They sing about that in the song, being homeless and in a situation that looks so hopeless. That is what the song is about.

The girl that worked with me a long time ago, I let her listen to that song. She told me that she could come home with me. I happened to be having a barbeque with some of Tony's friend that night, so I invited her to come over with her children. She decided not to come over and told me that if she came over to my house, she would probably try to flirt with my husband and get him to help her. She said that she thought she could steal him from me. I couldn't believe that she would say that. She then said she wouldn't come over to my house and do that to me, because I was so nice and helpful. She told me that she couldn't do that to me.

After that I just tried to help her by talking to her. I told her that I have lived through what she was facing, and I was only six years old then. It was very difficult for me to find a way to live at that time. If I had anything, someone would take it from me. If I had any money, someone would just take it from me. I had nothing. All I wanted was to go to school. All I wanted was to have a friend, but I had nothing. I was very lonely and was by myself most of the time. Even with all my sisters and brothers and my adoptive parents in the house, I was alone. I told her that she needed to do the right things, the things that would help her children. I told her that if she stayed positive, and was grateful for the things she did have, her life would change. I guess I was hoping that I would hear my own message.

About three weeks ago, I talked about all of this with my sister. For all these years I have never talked about this with anyone, even my son. I asked her if she wanted to know why I was adopted, if she wanted to hear the whole story. I was curious as to why she never asked me about any of that. I told her that I feel like I have three sisters and two brothers, and that they were all real siblings to me. I told her how proud I was of them. I told her that my sisters and brothers were always very nice to me, and that our mom was the only one that was hard on me. I asked her if she saw that side of our mom, and she told me that she did. She told me that they all knew what was going on, but they couldn't do anything about it. It was just how it was. She said that they all felt like they were lucky to live through all of that, so I guess our mom did things to her own children too. We talked some more, and I asked her if she wanted to hear my story. She told me that our mom had told them all about why I was living with them, and it was pretty accurate. She did mention that Mom had a house and a little store in Vietnam, but I don't know if she remembered that I had to live in the store. I didn't ask her about that, because I didn't want to ruin our good conversation. I was just so happy that I had someone to talk to that understood how I grew up.

CHAPTER 22

We work. I have time to do this, and I have time to do that. I have time to keep running around. I think of the flower. It is growing in the mud. It is growing in the dirty water. It doesn't get any help. It doesn't get anyone to help it or care for it. But you know what? It is beautiful.

My English is not perfect, and my grammar is not very good. I feel that I really want to tell my story, so it will help others. If staying strong and believing in God has worked for me, it will work for others in the same situation or maybe even something worse. When things are at their worst, you have to do what is necessary to keep going. If all you have is a dirty piece of food to eat, you eat it. If you have no clean water, you drink some dirty water. But you know what? You are alive. You continue to stay alive, and you do whatever it is you have to do. I am a grown woman now, and I am happy. I have a beautiful son. So I say to you, be strong and you will find happiness in what you have. I am happy for what I have, and I thank God every day.

AFTERWORD,
BY HELEN

The dream I have for this book is to reach out and help make people realize how important it is to become responsible and loving parents. The only thing you should worry about for your children is whether they are happy or not. Happiness is in the human mind. So basically you have to educate your children with a warm heart. You have to guide them so that they have a rational attitude about money. In today's life, money is essential and sometimes measures the success of a person. But money is not all there is and should not be held in the highest value. Money and wealth are fragile, and sometimes you may lose them. It doesn't matter; they can be found again. But there are many things such as reputation, honesty, and gratitude that are so important, and when these things are lost, finding them again may be difficult.

Parents need to teach their children about relationships between people in society. Sometimes you have to give, and other times it is your turn to receive. Teach children at an early age that they need to be grateful and that they need to express that gratitude.

If parents see their children doing something wrong, or something that offends another person, they need to teach the children to admit what they did wrong and to humbly apologize. If you do something wrong, or do something that offends others, you need to do the same thing. The child will learn to be sorry and how to forgive. Parents need to talk to their children and explain these things. Pray to God that their children become resilient and strong. Always desire more than you have, but pay attention to your soul.

AFTERWORD,
BY LESLIE THOMAS

When Helen and I talked about writing this book, she told me that she could not read or write. I assumed she meant in English, so I simply told her to do it in Vietnamese and that it could easily be translated to English. When she told me that she could not read or write in Vietnamese either, because her adoptive mother wouldn't allow her to go to school, it just broke my heart. Education is very important to me, and even though I couldn't understand the logic of what she was telling me, I knew at that point that it didn't matter: I just had to help her tell her story. I bought her a recording device and listened to hours and hours of her story.

Helen's continued strength throughout her life has changed me. Listening to her story has helped me to realize what is truly important in life and has strengthened my faith in God and in myself. Her story has taught me to prioritize my life, to do what I truly love to do, and to always remember that I am here to serve others. It has taught me that judging others is a useless endeavor, because we should accept others as they are.

For these things, I cannot repay her, but I am hoping that this story will help her to realize her dreams and allow her to continue to inspire others, as she has inspired me.